Perihelion

Also by Sarah Law:

Bliss Tangle (Stride, 1999)

The Lady Chapel (Stride, 2003)

Perihelion

Sarah Law

Shearsman Books
Exeter

First published in the United Kingdom in 2006 by
Shearsman Books Ltd
58 Velwell Road
Exeter EX4 4LD

www.shearsman.com

ISBN-10 0-907562-82-5

ISBN-13 978-0-907562-82-5

Copyright © Sarah Law, 2006.

The right of Sarah Law to be identified as the author of this work has been asserted by her in accordance with the Copyrights, Designs and Patents Act of 1988. All rights reserved. No part of this publication may be reproduced, stored in a retrieval system, transmitted in any form or by any means, electronic, mechanical, photocopying, recording or otherwise, without the prior permission of the publisher.

Some parts of this book have previously appeared, or will appear, in *Cafewriters* (online), *The Paper*, *Shearsman*, *Stride Magazine*, the anthology *The Allotment: New Lyric Poetry* (Stride, 2005), and *The Tabla Book of New Poetry 2003*.

'The Baptism of the Neophytes' first appeared as an electronic chapbook at *Mudlark*, www.unf.edu.mudlark/ in 2000. The version published here has been revised.

'Train of Thought' was first published as part of a project with the Norfolk & Norwich Festival Fringe, 2000.

The publisher gratefully acknowledges financial assistance from
Arts Council England.

CONTENTS

A Clutch of Monsters
Fake	11
Duellist	12
Spare Part	13
Pepper Pot	14
Stone	15
Fetish	16
Chivalrous	17
Evolutionary	18
Dignified	19
Parisian	20
Vegetable	21
Curious	22
Illusion	23
Plastic	24
Stupid	25
Primordial	26
Quark	27
Invisible	28
Hot Potato	29
Psychic	30

Death of a Visionary	33
Perihelion	34
Aphelion	35

Tai Chi Sketches
Parting the Wild Horse's Mane	39
White Crane Spreads Wings	39
Play Guitar	40
Repulse Monkey	40
Moving Hands Like Clouds	41
Fair Lady Works at Shuttles	41
Step Back to Ride Tiger	42
Snake Creeps Down	42
Sweep Lotus	43
Dragonfly Touches Water	43

Heritage	45
Forecast	46
Page	47
Flare	47
Silk	48
Quicksilver	48
Savings	49
Prynne Knows My Name	51

The Baptism of the Neophytes

Angel to Soul	55
Soul to Angel	56
La Maestà	57
Trasferimento del corpo di S. Marco	58
Una Sibilla	59
Crocifisso di S. Giovanni	60
L'Adoration dei Magi	61
Pietà	62
Maddalena	63
S. Francesco riceve le stigmate	64
Nascita della Vergine	65
Madonna del Rosario	66
La Primavera	67
Morte di S. Francesco	68
Noli me Tangere	69
La Madonna del Magnificat	70
Apparizione dell'angelo a Zaccaria nel Tempio	71
Battistero — Cupola sopra l'altare	72
Sposalizio della Vergine	73
Les Sciences Sacrés	74
Creazione di Eva	75
La Pala d'Oro	76
Ospedale degli Innocenti	77
Una Sibilla (2)	78
Madonna di Crevole	79
Ultima Cena	80
Presentazione di Gesù al Tempio	81
Madonna in Maestà	82

Madonna del Voto	83
Nozze di Cana	84
Madonna dagli occhi grossi	85
Madonna della Misericordia	86
Ritratto d'un signore nel suo studio	87
Trasferimento della Casa Santa	88
Capriccio of a Colonnade	89
Annunciazone dell'Angelo a Maria	90
Il Tributo	91
Allegoria della Chiesa	92
Mary Awaiting an Answer	93
Sea Lover	94
The Baptism of the Neophytes	95
The World's Your Lobster	97
Give and Take	98
Headache	99
Reality Principles	100
Pet Sitting	101
Saint Teresa Contemplates her Futures	106
Some Excuses for Leaving Early	108
Rubber Club	109
Cat's Cradle	111
Meditation Topics for Women	112

with thanks to Katie

A Clutch of Monsters

for Neil

FAKE

You ancient doll. Your wax film of a face
careers across the living room and fills
my vision. I am caught in a breathless womb,
pulse at the plastic yoke your body builds
and am hungry for clouds. I think we sit in rows,
half-hearted as the smoke seeps under doors,
hedging the onus of more leadership. I won't
if you don't first. Misery's twin. My friend.
In shops or in the chapel it's the same:
everywhere an idol doing nothing in the finery
of death. The glass cracks in the dawn and scuppers
defences of pepper spray, rock salt, dew;
and what you feared to love was what you knew;
they offer me a twist of daffodil.

DUELLIST

Burnt bird in a rich fruitcake. Your block
is in unlocking universal gestures; bad seeds spiral
in the trickle of evil grease you use to oil
phantoms, seasons. Blame the lonely malcontent.
He wants what has intrinsically been lost. The inn-
ocent intent of speech has got all bent, and I
daren't engage. My attitude is nude; I join
the stranger on his quest. And then the fiddle is
within myself, love griddled on a disc, all
my doing if the power shorts us out, not all
my friends condone the bleach, the whiteout segment.
A patch, a yin-yang pattern in a cup; the black
is part of therapy, smelling of wretched ether,
cuts a desert dash, my own flash choice.

SPARE PART

I have a precious metal lover. He's a child of ice,
wearing brands about his stubborn body. I
hoover up the splinters from his tomb, use them
to cut a new name on my arm. Into your vein
the snowflakes flow. You stretch and lumber along.
It's later, I'm watching the box and my dress slips down,
and everything puckers. Don't replace the part,
whistle for rats, or aggravate a war: I siphon
blue fluid and watch your small heart float; Mr
electric circuit, you're a jerk. Fist on the console,
sympathy's an allergen, an unscrewed iris, your
attitude's enough to block a lift shaft. Let's
do it in the tunnel with that time bomb on your back.
Credits crackle, rolling on in silence.

Pepper Pot

A blistering hump rolls over the hill.
Stasis commands us. I'm hooked. I can't move.
You fall and are booked by a terrible glare. This
is my nightmare and its residue. Here, a stalk
is the sum of fatality, waving crazily under a hat
that's cast by a boffin, a dodger, a mystery man:
my job to try and follow if I can. And you communicate
essential supremacy to these young worlds, herding
slaves up your radioactive tower, down your burning chute.
Once we were perfect. Dictionary race. And then
you put your finger on the one invented word,
released the raw body of a sword, lay
sweating in the rupture of projected end-it-all:
two live wires, in hands that never touched.

STONE

Must live. Calcified god in your anchorhold,
one cracked hand is brooding under rubble,
cupped to receive the breast of a companion.
Take my form into your fractured strands, and
bloom like coral. I'm captivated by your crystal hips,
see how we fit, the one into the other. Tessellation of desire.
We move through the chemical nave and are wed,
policy documents swimming in the cloud. But love—
your lips leak an alien language, your rough-shod
frequency pierces my temple; I fall out of faith.
Your carbuncles accrue, your middle thickens, I
can't see myself in the glitter so trip to the void,
force you to roar for that old bliss of empire, lost
to a thunderous grace on a once proud screen.

FETISH

Skull rapping vision. Pulse in the waste of time,
pinch it in, hit me with it. I remember a child who stood
before the glass cabinet, that Neanderthal cranium
soothingly irrelevant. Not so now, the archetype is
singing, this scientist gleams at the crux of taxonomy:
it all comes in time. Threaten as your face contorts,
your palm stuck to mine, no wave of a king on his mission
to resign. Fall to the floor and declare your idea.
All these people get the message, circle my skins,
think I'm sweet. Out of my golden lids destruction pours.
Remember me once, twice, as your vintage, my sleep
is almost as endless; wrap me in billows and bags
and I'll brandish a rock solid amulet, crumble you,
dunk my gestalt in a hot witch's brew.

CHIVALROUS

Your reverberations are unique. They pain
the arc of my ribs where the memories crowd
and flood. Two axes rear and strike, slow pro-
grammed to hold sense in abeyance. I slide
through a mirror; my skin gives the lie. Those
knights are slumped in cobweb glamour, we
are caught in the spell and tongue each secret,
each drugged wafer, turn in the slot of
gothic bodies, craving enslavement. My echo
is prophetic. Your toppled goblet spills the deal,
and what I learn from you is only real in stark
white transit. Blast this need to move beneath you.
I'm weak. I raise a war against the gateway,
fantasising how you'll slam me down.

EVOLUTIONARY

Look at how I try to talk to you. Spindling
fingers at the collar of your body, eyes
green and gleaming for a meal. Lover, you step
aside and raise the standard. How your faith
is solid and platonic, shielding me. But I'm polluted
into becoming young again, the blue pool
swirls through slits of time and punishes us.
I wish I'd said. I wish I'd said the word.
Thus a combustion and the slur of tears.
Marbles roll out of my unpacked bag. Sand the plane
and fit the windows in my ball and chain.
Now listen to my attitude of doubt; it liberates
a louche desperation. Gills and gasps proliferate.
I try to surface after it's too late.

DIGNIFIED

Noblesse refracted in the scale of grace,
you fighter with an icy mercy. I desire
to join your ranks. I'm grateful for my exile,
tuned to a dance on the moon's crater,
transported in a solitude. Tones signal
your masked arrival, and I turn the corner,
utter the conquered word. Your fabled force
is bliss on my skin, as I slip the noose of thoughts,
float in the air, enact an attitude of trance.
Who's the master after the fact: that foam
slathers the earth as you thirst for home;
and take my snowy back as further proof,
and clutch the pick of fractures from the past,
and chill me like a relic in a glass.

PARISIAN

Darling, you are divided like a king.
The art that kept these centuries intact
copies for us now the vital moments.
You, in your suit, crash-landing in ink
as each woman wrings her hand, reflects
that the dive has nothing on a platform,
a roundly stopped clock, a schoolgirl's hat.
There's a chicken in the basement.
Nothing is stable. Ascetics are marching
through this sumptuous city, arresting
silvered eyes and swathes of waist.
One day you order this; a genius paints
my face in afterglow, and your wealth is sealed
in this room with its bloom of hidden veins.

Vegetable

My heart is crushed. My mouth is full of juice.
Machine-pulped, each dumb fruit is concentrate,
each pressure point adds water to the mill, and you're
a cabbage with a mind to kill. Here's a symphony:
gloves twisting the buttons, a suave insanity of manners,
a thug, a knave, a girl. A ring around the wrist is like
a sentence, far from the world's bright hair,
and you tether me to your bad plans, ecstatically.
Out of the arctic comes your carousel, you feed it meat,
and I spit in your eye. The hybrid movement starts
to roar, and all the blades go green, and you imagine
another earth, where language is so much thatch,
dry and combustible under nature's slick;
helpless, deathless, fodder for thunder.

Curious

Light relieves me of my energy. I had
been moving in a lonely household, one
maid's persistent dusting motion, quarantined.
Now I am rigid in the splayed blast; all my stripes
bled out to a sign on a page; my belly pinned
through the softest part, my eyes cut gems of art.
He costs my make up, then he snaps me shut.
Just imagine the edges of his frenzy, its moving
halo, bloody, contracting his vision,
intrinsically threatening the status quo.
No wonder his cloak's electrified — a fence
around a turbulent osmosis. Your control
will grow to be a lady again, and all her rays
quiver in the crux of a live setting.

Illusion

I'm playing chess with the dark.
I've a bishop, a moated tower; and everywhere
the power of life and death. Take a stifled breath.
Make a move. This place on the outside looks too green
for a bowl, a stone, a master of possession.
Your agon inflates like a snake and is chanted down.
There's a germ in your crown. It makes teeth bleed,
the tongue flicker at the slide of a draught,
and I'm over you. Deaf and blameless as a crystal ball,
the girl trips, is saved by a centre part, stands still.
Why did I cast you? I thought to distort the box
that beats with irregular time on its wide arc,
flecking pleasure with a simple wisdom.
Discerning a hidden pattern, you shake me up.

PLASTIC

A polymer affinity is back. Blending
with the shadows on the market of your art,
dolls are made of you. Letters are bleak bodies,
conjuring industry, deputising androgens,
taking the place of command. While you're heaving
in the tank. It's an answer to attack. Drop the wrist
and roll those O's, release your trigger of a chair,
your evil troll. I'll paint it crudely shut, this draw
of the viscous tooth and claw, your mud conglomerate,
unmastering me. Then I look to the angle
of your magnetism, the collar, cuffs, scrape of the chin
on a brick wall. Look at the edge, the steep end.
Sleepless me. I've cornered the gadgets, the moulds,
I'm pressing a love from the air's hot soup.

STUPID

This grim lumber through time's tunnel.
Half a mind, a taste for betterment, and I'm
anyone's slave. Inset the jewel and cast your words
aside. I'll follow. Flat-batteried tram.
I grin if I'm borrowed; mind sliding under
resistance, the swell of a sculptured chest
or the streak of a shock. I like an army on the march,
I guard the porch. I smell of withered wreaths.
You say I've an affinity for sheets, and so
I rip and smooth earth's corners, tuck you
into a crush, pale lady. I don't understand.
You talk to the shape of where your master isn't,
reprimanding him for slips of faith,
spooning the ground, discovering its lip.

PRIMORDIAL

Touching the core makes your follicles discharge
a whiplash each. I envy you your skin,
you're immune to insults, bullets, kisses now.
You're like a Russian monk with a mad plan,
fingering jewels that glow in the stark
excavation of a violated grove. My roots
can more easily transplant than I'll admit,
unwillingness configures as desire, when
the life signs shift. You take the stairs. I'll make
the air that oxidises your complaint incur
a fatal fusion. Risk my neck to fit.
They say there's medicine stuck in the spiral,
luck glued to anger, splitting prison walls,
a terror that there's anything at all.

QUARK

Gold waves on a main frame.
Polluted baby voices on the run. My love
is appearing as a dimmer molecule
than chance would have it. Smaller than a doll.
There's a spice to what you smile and serve:
it doesn't seem a long time since we landed
in this quarrel, bolder after the smooth flow of sand,
grit in your veins. These charmers are the riddle
of a blizzard, are the blips that chart your heat.
Your rays are like cardamom, little bitter pods
embattling you against the probable,
making me wonder if thunder wears a dress,
and all the reasoning under the sun
can stop the burning savour of distress.

INVISIBLE

Never one to yield to a bleak welcome,
you tell me that this astonishing mist
shrouds a vacancy. I funnel the moist
and empty air into my lungs. A sweetness
settles on our hungry faces. It's wonderful
to sublimate life into a film; your world
a marble; memories like lace. You understand
the study that absorbs the well-wrought man.
I sidle lady-like into this place. The journey,
its planes and saws and fractures, terminates,
and newer lines emerge, loose as hair
flung over skin. Look at us, and shiver, and begin.
I can taste a space for incarnation:
gravity here is a transverse wind.

Hot Potato

Malice in your earth-bound dome.
You tether, unravel these prisoners, and
the shape of your mouth is evil. Lisp
a threat and the acres cower and quake,
experiments injected with your tread.
The pervy bully bandages enwrap me,
splice a chord of mutilating fear, so you
can see what drives and chases after minds,
like chopping knives. Like weights
pressing a saint into the mud.
I'm casting my dice for a military forfeit,
eluding your ambush, spearing your blind spot.
You nastily organised network of pawns.
I'm game to escape your drill.

Psychic

My own good nature eludes me; like a flash
in a fragment of mirror, an old bad thing
I might have done configures and distorts me.
You're a wisp of might-have-been, a thought
I have at night to ease paralysis. At this moment
zealous scribble could have timed me out,
elicited a let-down from a hook, productively
divided what I am. I draw a breath, and wonder
that there are so many left. We prodigy,
brought through intemperance to slavery.
Here I am then, singed at the skull, offering
a vision of the future. Slip a tower into a girl,
and she'll scream, disguise her hair as an old rope,
unravel herself. And close her eyes and hope.

DEATH OF A VISIONARY

It was the habit of her small, gnarled hands
to say the beads, to tell them daily
how through the freeze frame of a child's fingers,
a plethora of mothers found their forms. That woman
was as real as the dirt that bit their feet,
Lucia and the ragged siblings with her,
dirt they had no word for. Then that light:
a gold-edged spectrum in a dirt-poor night
and a voice that couldn't be heard. Only
her rose-lipped smile, her open palms,
snow white, vulnerable. In her face
such sorrow for the mud-stained human race.
The rest was fragile, intricate, like lace
for priests to press and sisters to unravel.

To see these things and live: that was her sentence.
The fragile wish of her bones for severance
tapped at whispers threaded together;
rumours of war. Fear. Rough cloth at the wrist.
A vision of the ministry of silence, bright
and overexposed. And finished. And much missed.

PERIHELION

The point in the path of a planet,
comet, etc that is nearest to the sun

Almost destroyed. But soaring.
I'm edging on my orbit to the raw
flare; singeing for the sake of it
my sky-tight lines. I feed my friends
into the fire; it's easy, first the distant ones
flung into vacuum, then my fly-by-night
acquaintances, and then the best ones,
all their loving mouths and outstretched hands
fluttering to charred oblivion. Won't you take
my body? Won't you shoot me through the heart
with big red flames? How flammable I am.
see how you've charged the structure of my skin
with sunspots. Thunder. Ardour. Hydrogen —
please — burn me up, according to your plan.

Aphelion

The point in the path of a planet,
comet, etc that is farthest from the sun

Stretched on the wrack, tormentor.
I'm pulled blue and skeletal, the fronds
of a huge collection of despites and attitudes
all vanishing. A track hid under snow.
It's part of the course of searching high and low
for starlight, and some evidence of you.
And in the stillness of these farthest days
your icicles and fingertips amaze me
with the vague persistence of a memory,
a shivered piece of guesswork. What I think
of all this great life cycle isn't here;
I can't resolve the elements, I'm scared
to add a drop of passion to the mix—
I might flow back to where I can get fixed.

TAI CHI SKETCHES

Parting the Wild Horse's Mane

I flex on your neck, High Stepper.
You streak the length of a flank, a taut
bow of the stars in their fire formation,
pulsing. Two snorts in the wardrobe,
luck in the heart, gas in the lock
of your bone-long jaw. I think
you must have been hit by a master,
someone in leather, their fingers in leather,
stabbing at sugar and velvet. As a child,
I fed a horse, pushing my vulnerability up to the arm,
for a mouthful of grass. You protected me then,
exhalation of dew on a plant, the gloss
of green leaf, a fairy story. Now
I'm scooping the waves of your grace apart.

White Crane Spreads Wings

Enormous love, however do you stand,
balanced on a fine illumination. I
mimic the time line, intangible, proud,
and so easily mislead. Once there was dancing,
blood, as if drunk from a tumbler, unravels
the good dark of an opaque pond. Blood
salts the snail, threads the corners of jaws,
is the secret hiss of a dream. Lift up your ribs.
Bliss like ice is the chain of a swing.
I really want to know: if I snare
the oxygen and find it's made of words,
split the similes and find white walls,
could you shred our blanket, break these eggs,
kiss me like an Eskimo — and soar?

PLAY GUITAR

You're blue in the distance, maestro.
Every body a sliver, each life a bag
unzipped in a wind machine, label-less.
Prayer like a zephyr and weeping as rain:
then a transposition, subdominant, and
a third, and a fourth, declaration of love.
Wash and slide on the resonant earth.
Every body makes mistakes, all thumbs
and sinister steps, the substance of a chorus.
Moodswings blister this manuscript.
Better the offer of plywood for the heart,
a cross of wires on your punctured hand,
a stool for your foot, and the other—
I measure the miles with plucked-out locks.

REPULSE MONKEY

This boy will steal your peanuts.
Sit for a minute, your eyes are gone.
Turn your head and the scrabbling at your neck
slips to your shoulders, breasts, the rest.
Lovely chatter pinches at the brain.
Nip me in the bud before I burst
with the injustice of hot weather,
the streak of a storm on the collarbone.
To break the cycle, push the inner lining
of holy robes down a kaleidoscope,
so that its saffron splits into cells,
empty segments smarten to a suite,
and a whole house blooms in a cage
(monkeys trampolining on a feather).

Moving Hands Like Clouds

You vague darling. Meet me in the pub
where the bad beer sprays out acronyms,
casts a pall over this dreadful air, where
arms brush fallen apples to their nests.
Then there's a flock of wasps, engaged
in soccer, in the spit and buzz of prey.
What do you think of this? You hardly know,
puffing dirty smoke over our tracks,
pips in crevices. Tendrils in the throat.
I love the gilded loss of autumn, where
my sadnesses are squirrels in the bank,
take a look, pitch a squint, reach back
through unsublimated meekness: coin
the *disparu* of all these arty cottages.

Fair Lady Works at Shuttles

Oh I bet she does. Anything to break
the mind in its insistence on derision,
the warp and weft of anguished indecision
made clean and attentive as cotton. My
prince lies in a dungeon with the sweats.
His double is crowned king. He'd marry me,
but then my head would spatter on a post,
my unwatched body turning perfect host,
white and gullible with frozen fingers.
Instead I fret the loom and augur sleep
as a pattern to impersonate. But lift,
and swift as darts your courage hits my nerves,
and I ring for my maid. She comes smoothly,
all curtseys, and buttons me up.

STEP BACK TO RIDE TIGER

The blur of your outraged maw, buster,
enervates me. I have to take a still,
swallow it down with exposure to limited risk.
Look there, flashless, framed against a rainbow.
My flesh glows hot at the very thought.
Part the feelings from the forewords,
and there they stay, in the mould of a key,
aching for ultimate power. Speed
is a loop for your pressure to trigger,
and I badly want that planet. Encircle
my neck with fur, my throat with gold,
and birth is a saddle I've flung away
with the whip of a rock. Bear up,
for this tornado will deliver.

SNAKE CREEPS DOWN

Your chunk of browning fruit lies on the ground,
slinky reader — want to check the leaves,
kill the chicken for his prophecy?
Whatever — it's the same twinge in the hip,
the crazy slide, the knotted hole-in-one.
I tried to rake the soil around the bones,
the wishes and the fractures and the lice,
little shudders of past romance. Flick
your book, the pictures speed into a trance,
and I like that. Keep lowering your tone,
and whisper what you learn. In gravity
the falling apple cultivates the grand,
the thousands of lab mice venturing on,
as eager as an unforked, salivating tongue.

Sweep Lotus

You have to make your own way home,
I'm sorry. There's some brushwood in the post,
blue touchpaper in your back pocket,
and a full moon tonight. My desires
are succulent petals, honey-covered—
not that you can stop me shedding blood.
There's a green tinge to our love, you see,
and infrared can verify your moves,
as you circuit the pool, packet of crusts to hand,
wondering whether the mythical bird
will come tonight. I ate too much
of the wrong plant, and winter gained
a painful lace, and now I need to stay here,
keeping the elixir for myself.

Dragonfly Touches Water

You make love to this moment. Quiverful,
the silence of soft water, not an answer.
Each stroke is a pellucid universe, a crystal
drop in the web, a planet made of chances.
Words pierce back into the breeze. I
laugh when you cast your throw, in deep
as an arrow, a slim electricity of swords,
the form of a warm embrace. Your subtlety
enters the imaginative ground, and breaks
cold surfaces into an opulence.
See how each prism echoes your soul,
the join can hardly be counted, all the
cuts we caused each other are bright streaks:
a quill pen under the fan of her wing.

Heritage

The first woman was Selima.
Her fingers were delicate. Four of them tapped
the tanned skin of her arm. The number of children
she would have was as yet undetermined.

The other hand played with a pen — a crude, scratchy
implement. Her thumb pulsed it forward.
Her fingers feathered it back. The lashes
on her closed eyes were innumerable.

Later, she waved the pen as if conducting
birds or the chatter of homecoming men.
She gathered the beats of their swift, irregular notes.
She shaped them into a roundness, a ringing.

I count the Selimas in their rooms, like lights
in cells. She circulates the body, sustaining, pearly.
Write her system down. It decorates, intricate
wedding henna on your unpledged hand,
alight on the moving branches.

FORECAST

There is danger in these waters.
You don't believe the tide could drag you under, but it does,
with the burning pull of salt,
with a planetary power.
You feel your feet, calves,
the skin behind your knees begin to sink,
your body's a soft edifice dissolving
and your mind's not what you think,
but something dearer
whose cast is Neptune, Jupiter and Mars;
the vast shoal of your longing
is shredded, then dispersed into mute strands,
and your heart's a single starfish
running rings, in an eternity of sand.

PAGE

You fetch your book and make me read to you.
I let the brutal images collide
in the mesh of the pain you sketch,
your knife moves quickly over blanks
piercing the skin that separates our mouths.
I'm an uncut parable to you, a strange cry
ripe to spill at a bruise of these dry sheets.

FLARE

Night visions of you rustle in my veins,
I dream, alert to every constellation.
I trace your profile onto songs,
twisting in the middle of my bed,
like the heart within your body.
The future leaps and shudders, I start up—
bow and arrow pointing at the sky.
We hunt each other, and I don't ask why.

SILK

Grace comes through your eye,
though I shrink like a sister behind canvas.
Green and white lilies silken my fall;
I know how to knot them, and lie
immune to the news, and twist
myself around, a body fit for sleeping.
I could grow quite easy, imagining
such a peaceful rending.

QUICKSILVER

Last night you fed me with fragments of sky.
The moon slipped down my throat so readily,
dispersed in my chest's thin vessels.
You made my skin shine. Then you pressed
soft black cloth on my aching mouth,
and eased the cuff of language back,
thirsty for silver in a dirty vein:
and what you opened starts the game again.

SAVINGS

I recycle
the words
that I find
on the street

They glint
with promise
like loose change

If no-one's around
I scoop them up

If I'm in company
I do it too,
for a laugh
but if I'm alone
in a crowd
I'm too proud.
The words
bulk out my pockets.
At home
I spill them out

And switch
each element about
copper
in this tin,
silver
in this. Until

Each vessel
is choc-ful
a reproach to me.

Small change
I could spend

on newspapers and
niceties and
milk

or slot
in pots
for charity.

Instead
I sit here, miserly,

a tower
of denarii
pressing
on each eye.

PRYNNE KNOWS MY NAME

It hangs like a calligraphic hinge
within the recesses. Dark and astigmatic,
the act of naming shivers a release. In
with the pin-prick of a chance; informal
splicing of regality, contextualising knowledge.

It is the fuming of a censor swung through
the plunge of agnosticism. Counting the slow
beats of a carpet song. Clinging, my difference
to the black jacket of singular stance, against
all laws of residual shlock (and the hourly glance).

He knows the counterblast of appetite.
Slops on the directory causing stuck words,
lost chronicles dashed with young blood,
lung flood, and a small white scroll issued
with aplomb. Script-lash is more than enough.

THE BAPTISM OF THE NEOPHYTES

ANGEL TO SOUL

(I wanted this to be condensed.)
You love the thought of me lying
prone and unselfconscious
on the borderline of sleep;
your mind, now foul with cigarettes
now washed completely with remorse
wants to cut reality at root;
transplant the intensity of days
to a sweeter breeze
as I dream you lift the chord
to frequencies that shatter
and poetries that feed;
only you're still cherishing
modern introductions
to those age old texts
slipping on the point of sacrilege
(I love the thought of you daring)
the retreat to enrapture:
we're always doing it,
waltzing the subliminal around

Soul to Angel

I'm fatalistic about disappointment,
the fact that one day it may fade,
this room in which I knew I'd find you;
all the small sufficiencies of faith
fractured into derelict desserts.
You're away now, slowly resigned
to ulterior subsistence, pocketed
by ghostly partnerships, aligned
to re-characterisation as lack
and the absence of softness on edge.
I'll storm thought, my preparation
course, studying how best to please
imagistic hokum, the retorts
gleaming in idleness, spelling
admiration, amber, doused alone.
There is an arrhythmia to longing;
systole and diastole, low leaps
up to a clean fluidity of hope
spoiling the immunity of ice,
arrowing over these grey clouds.

La Maestà

Today quaked into a good age.
Rushes are cut to middle men, sticking
jewels to flight of robe, feeling
velvet lines of succour more than hope.
Beings gaze demurely over edges
while a mother sees us out, soft
hands like limpid answer after doubt;
dubbed unswerving of a custom's cloth
spilling favours even as we lean
to an earlier representation, to largesse
of slight withdrawal from full flesh
finding a field of stillness, through guidebuzz
of weltered elbow and deleted fuss.
Somehow, she's the turning poignancy—
deliquescence of iconostatic applaud
and shades of sumptuousness to come
—as the sun self-indicates biopic
(wings around the dislocated column)
and a hatched sheen of my becoming
votary, magnificently veiled.

Trasferimento del corpo di S. Marco

Three men and a body in a boat—
that Gothic glint in the eye, small-drawn
arc, covering a vow, slow-bound
sea a translucent hayrick, leonine
mane devolving from an epic voyage.
I see a face imprinted on the portico,
remember the press of tongue
inordinately pointed to a city, strange
pull and draw of water, after hours
drinking cordiality of books
built to besiege, precariously, a craft:
collapse of a curtain, as we spread our arms,
roping round the body's lyricism
rousing sainted reverie—alive!—
soused in fortune like a pantheon
(the dry world parties), oared
as theotokotic missioners; waving,
continental fellowship marooned
in a thrice-illuminated dance: high
eloquence, in sailing for a chance.

Una Sibilla

Hark back to the testing days.
You made your mark in the sky
throned on cloudsplayed rays.
Thought is a curdled belt, informing
serenity of a shapely waste, of timed
reflux of mentality. Speak out.
solid knees always dazzling
professional etiquette throughout a line
of brow-stressing, or depressing, truth;
darting spear that punctuated hair.
Not your habit to writhe fascistically,
wring the blood of stigmatism, flout
a story. Yet the parchment quenches
a studious thirst for prayer, benevolence
for enamorata in the stalls. Which woman
stills the benched pedestrian, lost
for nation and quotation, lowered head
in commuted wisdom, lunch tone:
I'm a mere visitor, entranced,
your fingers charge the air.

CROCIFISSO DI S. GIOVANNI

Bearing sickness was sorely wanted
in a place of fashionable death
and the rent of his abjection. Bow
your head, inflamed contentions, clots
of reason bloodying the branched belief.
The road sears eyes, rasping to an end
respiratory battle of night, stillholding
Spiritus who grasps a shadowcloth;
still I fear to take you in my arms
before the masses trip to ridicule.
Streets denying warfare, platitudes
surprise a deepening (we weren't to know)
the inexplicable invades the home—
count the rhymes I let you make,
cold bleat of eastor-in-the-dark;
face excruciates face.
My gaze is a remorsed bruise,
a breast swollen with empathic grief
incurve of fingers, candles, dames,
suffering beggars the frame.

L'Adoration dei Magi

Render me jewels with a green sheen.
We're honoured by a length of light
and martial grace of coordination
impacting town upon town;
and who is sick of reading on the ride?
Depend upon a loose leaf
tree art languishing in stellar clime,
sand carpets trace out a function:
you owe me, that's fine,
or dump the land I mine;
lad drops flakes on an open page
child upturns the rosy beaker
kisses as the cash floods back.
Donkey scrapes the literati's arm
weightless polars ice the earth
in your tight fist, in your wish list
a sibilance my foot won't tread
up rival tower, up river bed
a frank and thorough fantasy,
a sober place to lie.

Pietà

They undertake a threnody,
two women and one God, losing
slavery of bones, of muscle-tone.
Mothering, her purest hair is white
weaving satchel and sarcophagus
to perambulate the drift of grief,
dead-legged, lost-twisted,
celestine withdrawal, into mist
the mouth that moved, half carved
palliative redundancy, the temple
should have prepared for this; flaw
in the prime, wax man, sun burn,
an uttering rib. Somehow the figure
sustains our balance, trapezoid
fibres hooked and lifting
scapular thrown into station
bypassing arterial hope, breathe
labouring bread on my scalp—
there is no point, there is no way
I saw the flames upsurge

MADDALENA

Remorse is circulated by a blade
splicing veins of pleasurable nature:
drain and outspill the guardian of self
torture is the illumination of cold air
stumbled on granite, alien root
suborning species through fine comb.
How the days staunch desire's lost letter
and digital impress grey-fades
to a prison, remembering bleeds.
You are crazy in the sun, blushing
like a hooligan with flowers, just
a genius, canvassing passion, where
truce silently hollers, detains,
encrusted with my fruit, dried
and needed for victuals, singsong
and rituals, a generative war.
Purity is a voided featherbed
a tumbled fanatic remaining aloof
and stubborn in the clasp of fire
of a type, for the woman, of truth—

S. Francesco riceve le stigmate

A mermaid, sublimated into shards
of ethereal glow, embryonic on the side.
Cartographer, sweeping plants along
inchways, measuring the martyrgold;
a stolid friar and dour worm of habit,
limbos on the hook of iridescence
while the new world folds, cobbled
into a jig of gravity, upstarted.
His aureole enrobes a bed of nails
catalogued as *Laudem Gloriae, Dulia,*
hypostatic as the honours raise stakes,
thrilling trails of platelets, corpuscles
nestling into myth, the place that waits
slung through a ring of planets. Palms
bedecked with parachuted threads
on which floats mystery, awarded
for historical agendas of fragility
your hypnotic reticule of scent;
intimate to me the woundedness of art,
the soundings of an unmapped start.

Nascita della Vergine

Hooded eyes as if to seize the crown;
apprehension welded into suavity
monitoring the temperate profile, all
those goblets of the past, peremptory
in animation of her throat. Push
is the one commandment, hankering
for a return to soft sands, in an hour's
shift of secrecy. This room hesitates
to insult, is coaggrandized by a split.
She'll hear the cord, the pacey
end of it. A chip of intelligence
sours his tea, the fancy, partycoloured
weightlessness of office, becalming
a martial arsonist, subpoenaed friend
grazed by choke-manoeuvres, home
ragamuffins, the lithest hands around.
Reading out her sobs, naked, lies
an abundancy of solar aptitude. You
guess my smothered age, uptight
the moment evens out a human right.

Madonna del Rosario

Take me out with berries of redemption
your final style of interludic racing
dis-ease of connection is raw,
falling into single trance, kissed
in a cobalt memory, unpeeled cell
of attraction, the chemical wonder.
I'm cryogenetically squandered, I
crumpled my chance. Didactic élan
feeds as a drip my intent, altruism
lining coves, passion's wick
and the infinite pain of the cast
volume. Bear's shady torch, to claw
at that thick, manacled sagacity
intrepid in customising brands
(a looming tangibility of lack)
until my sainted call for you is feral,
trawled with compressed carbon,
making zones; antiphonal response
to this vacancy's torrent of blue
burnt ice, inner view.

La Primavera

The burgeoning elastic of my crime
hedging inconsequence. Renewal
defenestrates the old ties, a letter
to the man from holiness, sutures
on a darkened brow. I bought a bunch
in whimsical denial of the sluice
and psyche holographed in tears.
The arc of a shot vessel
curling slowly into blood
and rebirthed reminiscence;
spoon me sugar on the trolley
while we wait, modus vivendi,
tossing fagends on the map of
meanwhile, magnetical surfaces
shivering like telegraphs.
Every time I spit it out, a ghost
prances in the middle distance.
There are no qualifications for hope,
constellations slide in obduracy
plans elide your voice in kindly smoke.

Morte di S. Francesco

Erasure of intensity
featuring angels tonsured by despair
churning out their lachrymosal job
against sprung juvenilia.
Extremities still beckon
a carriage of nourishment
preceded by snow, stripped
of their unique devices
(stripped of their women):
tablature in dissolution
and deep field of drapery—
such a business of cowls.
One shaken fist, at the hieroglyphic
delegatory swarm. A riven disc
inked about a stone footrest
for oscular chiropody.
A barrel for the laity's design
wreathing the statuary line;
cover my mouth in humble exegesis
and testify to birdsong (it was his).

Noli me Tangere

Eidolon instransigent at dawn:
a girl producing ointment
it's true—your hands are larger
than my life; she's genuflective, only
tractable to the bloom of doves.
To contemplate the resurrected stride
unenveloped, thrusting, distinction
awaiting a new dispersal:
such intervals decree a loosening
of blooded society, ripped
through gasp of stark heart
to relinquishing; no tight grind
so still to fall. Forestlight, cellular
the fresco feel of compassion,
scythed or sceptred, sacramental
momenting of blaze, volition
collides with drench of voice
—I'm triggered by that word rejoice
like the moon, sylphing, swelling
into reflective choice.

La Madonna del Magnificat

A comet power-lifting from your nape
as filamented fingers play the grain
of running desert, ruined wall, scrolled
and retrograde as Venus. Softly ethered
solemnity of hush, a camel's calm
bathing again, in a lucid star, wed
to a stoppered gloss. Heliocentric,
the way light grows along a line
(burn of the shoulders, bearing down)
and tipped to butterfly elves
(the rasp and rattle of her mind)
as we choke on sopranos, sucking
miasma out of a night lawn. Splice
this tablet, that fleece-armed
memory of whose seraphic aperture's
daguerreotyping novices midheaven—
prana, chi, a subjective function
wharfed and whittled into glass, our
transcendental eulogiaic station
depicting layers of her auburn crown.

Apparizione dell'angelo a Zaccaria nel Tempio

Effortless decampment, his wand
intensifying pastures, woollen, dyed
through regal armature, the sullen
humidity of recital catching here.
The centenarians monitor your grin
as you sidle upways, moshing
sans alacrity, their worry-beads
offside; such firmness of thorax,
a density of Vinciesque cartooning
over the riven rock, frieze
and subtle luminosity of hours—
the ludicrous perspective, petalled
in selection after cagey bars.
He's ballading the gospel, she
native to his fugal directive,
loosens all sore cuffs. To ask
what happens in the evening
of a scheming hermeticist, redux.
People passing, ionising acres,
for the catalytic storymakers.

BATTISTERO — CUPOLA SOPRA L'ALTARE

Callipers engaging in *détente*
the throng stepping a grapevine
in small bursts, palmistry enclosing
the secret of ripe velvet, bitten
by a glimmered edifice of faith
plaiting the thoughtful star in dalliance
(pressing the thrones in flashlight)
an interview of vineyard graces.
I'm bashful: acknowledgment
is a walking wavelet, drinking
slips its plastercast, plays on
a parabola of syncopation, dome
charged with *apolytikion,* diurnal
welcoming of souls, and pearls.
Forbidden to kneel, flame in
a favourite cluster of faces.
Salt dances, preserves the draft
ameliorating the measured tread
ring of hallowed oil on head
the puzzle of circumference.

SPOSALIZIO DELLA VERGINE

Her peccadillo always was to soften
(arches of flamingos in the hall),
buttering carpenters a brioche
in a soothing monotone
whose chemistry would vilify
extremes of umbrage. Catseye
leaping into the near-hearted
enclave, a nymph triumvirate
hectoring at the old rigidities
as a swing of gender, stretched
with the humanity of temperature.
A yam's follicle, a soda sponge.
Marriage is a mantra, stirring
interstitial ore, rinsed, wrung
by happenstance and satin
countenance. Conquering malaise
they stealthily astonish the wretched
through a humidity of jugular
in fulminant *parousia:*
your boat-neck signifies a launch.

Les Sciences Sacrés

Flamboyancy gathers knowledge;
that efficacy in fighting the monstrous
through a shake of dust, a boom
of sonic cavity, clamoured ivy.
Chin in grip of rational advice
furtive in a generous disdain
of evidence; the pharmacy meridian
tough as a cluster of birds
assembling on the legendary bough
of baldaquin, of battlefield.
Who threw that medicine ball?
An antibalm, serrated prescription
condemning the small by design
to imperfected logic, overweight
by canonical procedures, evergreen
otherwise, a federation lawn.
A guru floats, a hermit prays
in all her microcosmic rays,
robes like spectra born of rain:
the universe expands again.

Creazione di Eva

Sacerdotal plunge into the flesh
splitting sides, in childhood bypass
freshnesses that can't be said
to be family, dysfunctional as
the natal organics of life
as he thought he knew it (walked
in the gardener's arm, waltzed out
as if from an arc, by two).
Satinate the stretch of skin
seeking gold of fallen robe
from gallant surgery. Her head
born like Venus from a shell of ribs
a foaming solo masterpiece of faith
as if you couldn't suffer enough
through a summons. Take part
of a plumed bird, gun-shot,
an unringed finger leaving out
no sullen multimediatrix
layering time, through foliage,
beckoning, a quizzical olive branch.

La Pala d'Oro

Is it wisdom, holding you in such
reverence, a costly liverage, salute
a million replications of a kiss
missed through a pull of honour
and eyes that blazed in numbness
as I touch you for another
and another spark, biting fear
on the sharp edge, exposure
never seemed easy as words
pooled into poisonous valour
or a nighted hatch, your length
a house of wood, slip courage
into my hands, at last, at all.
We never know the future,
obscure as other people, darker
than an initiation, replete
with echoes prophesying
tenderness, or trouble, pointing us
at an altarpiece, painted deep
in hesitancy and the need to leap.

Ospedale degli Innocenti

Consider my looks
as we touch covers
drawing from raffia significance
a legend of softness, interplayed
under orders to function as two
figments of history
consider my touch
as we look over
indeterminacy as a pledge
of some substance, delayed
while blood courses through
this fragile banality
consider the torch
the gleam of the forge
as air splits soil, condensing
moisture as novel elixir, a drug
speeding old speech to song
through which my elevated sense
seeks blue flames, signature,
a storming of the miniature.

Una Sibilla (2)

Your face is a rich fit.
There's luminescence, somewhere
in your background, a ludicrous stammer
leading to the moon's vocality,
a quiet dismissal of modality
as the solution in which to be born
and rise, smiling, into our creation.
Frustrated you might be, by the day's
stars, so I'm familiar with rawness
as tense questions bloom, tabled
by inventive elves, nourished
through catch of gossamer, entire
as life is entire, yet barely drawn.
You hand me questions openly,
The lightest trust, a weakness
in my pelt of defences. Brute joy
staggers the outcrop of your sleep,
adrenalin jewelling what you keep
in savoured vigil, waiting games,
the sudden linking of our names.

Madonna di Crevole

Reach for a thimble, a third
icon obviating all the striations
of preciousness upon the velvet
of your voice, the gesture of slowness
a roll of simultaneous pleasure
and nurture of the hazelnut.
Pallor isn't always tremendous,
a lack or splitting of unconsciousness
as the home you winter in, spread
at all the stimulants of flight,
shameless in the blow of night
or jacketed cheaply; you're vulnerable
to a title's allure, blonde rope
as the gateway, chastise me, elope
should predictions admit us
(on the cusp of climate change)
that wild extremity of joy,
charging the world, raptured
confluence leading my release:
your strange embrace of stranger peace.

ULTIMA CENA

Because I tried to walk away
tried to stalk the immobility of 'while'
proffering, withdrawing sympathy;
as the twist of snow dessicates harm
as the footsteps conjunct our stream
crassly, backing the chair, we'll waive
those terrors. Diurnal marathon
to succour love at all, whose rented room
alleviates the contract, coming down
to a proportional embrace;
there's a sense of grasping grace,
your visual entertainment, supermark
all the idle gossip of five wounds
and consequent insomniac despair.
I'm sorry, prone to emergencies
prioritising what's known to be familiar
sounding pain behind the doorless cell;
sense of that layout, sensing all too well.
Only this, instransigent and dour,
the brief resuscitation of a flower.

Presentazione di Gesù al Tempio

Bless the infant in the Trianon.
I am perfectly robed as I tell you
my dream of the marbles, my dream
the argument of nutrition, repairing
lost temperature, fluttering passcards
ever the mutual date obscured,
slipper into the colourful campaign
to bring us home. Fog's redundant
breaks not cleared, tea soaked
intimations under palms, sapphire
a hallucination of warranty
and the limits of giving. Please
notice the terrestrial interest
—though for all the skilling on the edge
you'd think me criminally gilt—
trace the elements of covert
kindness, too elementary
to long sustain elation, yet
I'd report the author of the plot
hoping little, reading you a lot.

MADONNA IN MAESTÀ

Plump with the reality of wonder
that ineradicable line of Greek
questioning her maker, filling out
the ponderous auricle of blessed
interregnum, smoothed design,
the clamour of impressed footmen
contrasting with brutality's dispassion
the road ahead, when a rage
of feathers heralded the seat.
All your education's now unique
and I long to be enlightened
by the fold of your thoughts.
Economies of spiritual connexion
dazed by a bold plan, we lack
a multitude of sanctions, budded
into greenery, yet ordained
to yearn for affirmation, high, higher;
spill like milk, a gentleness
waking up her body's stellar pride
our latent tangibilities collide.

Madonna del Voto

History flows wide of the mark—
it's days since I've conspired
for a quick resolution of the mime.
Calcifying smiles, features employed
in the passing of dusky pipes
which resonate the consort
as my spiral of early bones
knit their question, hallowing
an easy sextile of contented
harmony, unshepherded in skin
(the swells and contours intimate
as dark sides, split across this lake).
There's always an invitation,
hovering like harmony,
shuffled and aligned as charity
should you play that song, you'll
call the constellations to alight
cellars yielding drinkables
thinking that you'll percolate
a freezedried heart, in solemn birthday cake.

NOZZE DI CANA

Incidentally I found you
crossed at all the tender places
able to interpret glances
as the synonym of gifts
your attenuated smile
speaks to me in metamorse
all the richer through long quietness
and the intervals of weeks.
I would give you wine, should I
feel your thirst about my wrists
pulsing in an echolation
of the constancy of fits.
Incrementally I'll sound you
hospitable in small traces
ladelling the old romances
through the synastry of lifts
you're a suiter for a while
stealing on a burning horse
all these pictures of delighting
through the liquor of antiques.

MADONNA DAGLI OCCHI GROSSI

Conventional mortal thumbed and blurred
swimming in heterogeneous word;
hands are tender and delicate, feet
sullen shining clumps of no defeat.
I'm drawn to the reflective shoulder's velour
the no-pulled punches stare,
no time lost wincing to the side
to temper stolid features there.
The seat's for you alone, broad based
but backless, up to you to straighten
miasma of rumours, ostracised
into square-eyed flight, yet heard
as an autograph of the unknown
possibility of geniture. Leverage
in what rough-hewn artifice
blasts this lassitude aside
and I see us stunned by love's clasp
softened through the sifted wreck;
you were watching for a sign
large and tangled, gone off-line.

Madonna della Misericordia

Under your coat, cracked
mountain, I'm cramped
to the side of yearning. Sheer
timeline of kindling, annunciate
arcane fossils of becoming, show
them now, replete, dissolved
into a text; this red-hand verse.
Re-introduce a frequency
over the social buzz of strolling
life (the flimsy article), a name
shelved between schedules, dig
under downy platitude;
discover millennial injury, make
good the discovery, curl
treasures from revisionary dust;
orbit unconceivable souls
establishing a closer than
the middle distance, dance
into my skin, lighter
than sheets of addresses.

Ritratto d'un Signore nel suo Studio

Secrecy ascribed to vellum,
your keys are hanging everywhere,
traced by lizards, you're brooding
over what's faced by words
tabletop-scattered, sacralist,
tutored for an unlit score, serve
honourability on sufferance.
The letters distract you, declare
a supernature of the heart
though you'll take an age to learn
the difference of instinction
less the reason, than completion,
you'll turn with your forefinger,
fly me down. Cold air
afflicts like egrets, bitter, sweet,
I'm plummeting beneath your knees
or looping overtide, eventual,
a ruffled slit of silk, a spinning rag.
Check the paragraph, look back
to the night you felt that lack.

TRASFERIMENTO DELLA CASA SANTA

In the street, my dreams show up
cleanless, more alert to trouble
such as the blush of rages
peeling an extemporised allusion
to make you feel; at home
simple lavender attracts
accreditation as a navigator
through the boundless hours, thin
myocardial walls, contract, sign
in to inhabitation, outreach,
broadcast of a wasteland.
There's a flurry if we walk
in mackerel skies, thunder
scowls, interested, should this
turn into more than a turn
of primaries, flood sepia,
play about, a concerto
of retrenchment, even joy?
Intersect the rhythm of detention;
spy the transposition unalloyed.

CAPRICCIO OF A COLONNADE

Mathematics was never so pliable
as blossom leading to comfort of apples
the oar of a strophic victory
in soaking magazine pages.
Effortless, desultory, I'll flick
ash or lashes into line
(while I must not victimise
weaponry or aptitude
any shinng knight may do)
shrugging off patronage, to
bolt into arms, strong-spun,
you calculate something of infinity
ignoring your vacatory split
rowing through dense orchards
a resolution of armouries
mosaicing rings of Saturn.
A losing trade in meteorites
can't help your belief;
does this equation of the Grail
extenuate the plough?

Annunciazone dell'Angelo a Maria

The air connects us.
Friendship fires the line; it isn't
that I'm guided by this cut
I dreamt your heart sustained, whetted
in extraordinary pasts, all exes lost.
I'd rather scrub those garments
in your company, the suds rising,
sublimates of sentimental marsh
our evolution clarified. Drink to this
like lunar crystal sharding ice.
I'm pelted, you're volcanic.
Rotation of the arc, signalling
with beauty of its own, dangerous, swift,
coating dailiness with rays
that wait with tremor, and surmise.
The elements have history
the universe, an intimacy
as tangible as melted snow,
the thought of your home, our conversation
touching the fragility of music.

Il Tributo

Age is no deciding factor
as we reverse out of the slump,
bronzed in a flick of hair,
eyes shelled from their simmering.
The time of birth is a moot point,
some saying the flashpoint is all,
some that the pain haunts the castle,
rolling to an inevitable embrace.
I'm an exile standing at the window.
Office hours, internalised, personal
commendation of the forest,
(as the book hints, gaze at him)
a solitude that bleeds when taken there.
With sorrow's intention, weariness
lends a shrug to empathy,
we're substantially water,
plastered by fantastic colour,
a wall of erudition, by a mask
meant to protect those cherished lines
I learnt to stretch, by gut.

ALLEGORIA DELLA CHIESA

My attitude's no plenitude.
Hedging in and out, love's a maze
appointing no relief. Turn
your head, I could be sitting on a rock:
into rugged readers, loose belief.
Kindness half be-cottoned; stance
a gestural ambivalence like pain.
Hope fading out, then warming up again;
I can hardly kid myself we're home,
the tides reverse. Paths allotted burns,
tested histories alarmed to roost.
I long to hold a compass, take a charm,
unspinning damage, alleviating pressure,
in the lower zone, abrasions swarm.
Initiation's a damn, welling up,
lapping at a party or a dance
(haberdashery the main expense).
Overcoming opportune romance, daily's
the thing, the chasm, the deduction
from the lonely contours of this map.

Mary Awaiting an Answer

Waiting is women's work.
I don't imagine that you're sitting there,
picturing the wrenching touch of loss
or its converse, reddening at thought
of how sweat sings, and tears.
There's quietness in agony, a nothing
to be done, a darkening.
I think my face impassive, after
the fracture of separation, sudden
even though the end foresaw the start.
Rings do their work, and break.
My veil enraptures me. I'm still
a little slow to read (I tend towards)
your psalmic innuendo as a pledge,
—the time this seems to take—
our temperature failing to incite
release, or condemnation. I sit
tight, as loyal, as subject, to your grace;
the game of our unwinding
suffers me this corner of a place.

Sea Lover

You and I, gradually
interpreting that dance
we've practised, quietly, for years
as a stretch of grace
a loosening of lines
delineating your defence, or mine
I'm leading, though you set
the music breathing on my skin
(feetsoles exposed);
tautology of etiquette
demanding that we linger
on the boundary of touch
ambivalently signing
the willingness to risk
as in the choreography of chance,
your gentleness is dark
deferral of the flood
of enervated voltage
the chords between us sing
the light between us hurts

THE BAPTISM OF THE NEOPHYTES

The expression of your testament
flows skin to sublimate. Come here,
process until the plateau floods, and
time repaints that moment to the wall,
your mouth bruised with faith.
Life's torrential, a brush of flesh,
your collage of submission. You
can only push at love so much,
—spending rain in reparation—
thought that hurts confessed in free dimensions,
lifted through speech to the eye's
pigment, a touslement of fruit,
soft-eyed in tension's handling.
I'll read again our slow transections,
the critical refluxes of despair
harbouring innocence, a glance of light
wreathing narrativity
like velvet in the raw, you're
surviving the ache of smoke,
the fire that clouds us up.

THE WORLD'S YOUR LOBSTER

The world's your lobster, matey,
it's cherry red and biting,
and any assignation to the pot's

the lot of lobster plots. The
world's your stabbing ground,
magnificent shell of surrection,

curvaceious pincer movement of the sea
lobbed and bloated under
scarlet armour, the boated jester

making a song and slimy dance
of its ugly countenance.
The world's coasting by

on a stove of boiling brine.
Things to bring and sell, and always
the cold slab of the table after

the world's your oyster, darling.
See the grave wave of a landed
ladybird, crawling towards communion.

GIVE AND TAKE

He said to me, returning the book
on late Russian Orthodox saints,
'I've never read such fantastic words,
they filled my head with that just-right light,
the blue-gold shimmer of a peacock's tail
fanned into four dimensions (for time
is traversed by the languages they speak)
and nothing much has changed in my head—
but everything changed. As if the space
in the puzzle gently nudged my finger,
requesting that I set the letter right,
let the small space zigzag to the centre,
an empty point caressing our atoms,
silken filament blooming into vision.'

I said to him (having offered tea)
'You push against the boundaries
and phrases of civility; I think you must
have swallowed the gamut
of watering fowl, of nesting doves.
I hope you're writing it all down,
these fragments lost in fractured files.
I see your Adam's apple at work,
his loss of voice redeemed in time,
though powder makes your breaks snap off
and I love you nevertheless for that,
so all your wounded borrowings
I'd like to gather in my arms,
taking in faith the title you gave me'.

And then I placed it on my desk.
Its golden cover, cracked black spine
were absolutely irresistible.

Headache

My brow is blooming in rows of sweet
pea pod synapses. Tiny green tendrils
pulsing in the glimmer of the light.

Somewhere a word is trying to get through.
It's tapping on the membrane of a dream,
the liquid skin of an empty orb, propelling

an old air, a merry note, a dim reasoning.
Better get to bed on time. This will allow
the right sensations to push their roots

into the high-tog quality of my life. I had
too much, the slipper pain of that couple
before midnight, when I should have been alone.

The walks can't shift it, the limbering down
deludes it into vanishing; then there it is again
winking into sight, a fleck in the eye—

I feel the hot chocolate rise and slick over
my burning neocortex. Think about pills.
Remember your cool lips kissing me clean.

REALITY PRINCIPLES

The memory of my last journey is neither here nor there,
worrying at its own lack of track through words on the line,
through words out of line, through the falling of minutes
neither thick nor thin, heading undressed towards what anyone
deserves: an arrival, a fantasy rival, the screech to a stop. Your
love is disembarking from my body's clock. I could carve out the
space where I watched you watching me.

Dispersal of freedoms, flat waters, low wires.

The nerve of my gaze re-animates you, makes you jive like
jolting coffee in a cup. Don't drink, I'll exist before any blue dye
encapsulates the echo of my skeleton. You're raw as the fall of
a sparrow, shot for a lark. Don't flutter away. The takings get
totted up here: it's a one-flight stop, young nun, he hasn't a soul
in his pocket to speak of. Empty them all and continue to count,
pecking the dust.

An elegy for upturned telescopes.

Waving like a sound from the top of a tree. Spotted in a glimpse
of fairer weather. Adlestropping me from your quiet container,
loose in my hair. A clash of cultures, this stuttering buy, a first
purchase on the primrose path. To have or to hold, know angels
in their echelons of rank, and prophecy: a pot of cream for this
slip of time. Waving in concentric layers, your legs unsteady,
hardly there at all.

Pipette weather, precious grapes; peepshow.

The shadow of my body sullying the carriage. There's silver on
your skirt, a wrapper past its last; there's a speck on the glass for
punishment. I've previous experience at visiting the sick. Inky
finger, brow-beating the news. Read it backwards on my face.
Training the long lines, interpreting the rings. The loop in the
branch, tiny eyes, the hint of an escape — will it ever let us go?

Tightrope governess, coining a loose-leaf phrase

I approach with my mind wide open. The vortex of thoughts devolves upon your slide, the cell of ingenious screening; smiling, happy bubble. Irradiate me — with your possible existence: a spit, a polish, I'm full of potential. Prayers to a liminal artifice, prayers for a life. Feeding on conical data, I lose the microscope. Fingertips thirst for your resonant oil. Play a tattoo on the top of the table.

Squeal as the heart defines its destination

Justly yoked together, my speaking becomes the wall of your vision, mashing the senses, nourishing creases, plumping them up. I cannot tell what you were thinking before we came here; no Holmes, no deduction, you end up paying full whack. Or is there appeal to the limit of your currency, a large no-charge to the viewing of all these pretty angles (turn the corner and we've slid away from town like a postage stamp).

Snowflake credulity. Cover your head.

Polarity of travel frightens me. Concentrate (steep liquid) on the density of tickets, filling your schoolbag like a charity appeal. Slopping your findings down dresses, on best Sunday mentors, not caring for the scores. Kids' intensity striking a pose, finding the extreme position and flagging you down. Increased and aging velocity: I wonder if we ever had a childhood, ate candy, drew straws.

Worrying the label; gulp and dilute.

This map configures me as chemical. My homes are the bonds that place me where I am. I'm looking to pull you from the quag of indeterminacy, to give you a new name, sign you with a cross. There's hope in your carriage, tongues of air, blood, and, for all your talk of fire, a settling of skin. See the right man and your outlook could change. And I'm entirely horizon, call me sky, make me land.

Is it for you? Could it be for you?

Immense visitation. Sweeping through to the depths of hesitation. See me out: rank parallels of brick over brick, and the guards gone home, and the swinging letters suggesting penultimate traces. Pop goes the office, we're here for a fiver of chant. Can't get the parts though; can never get the parts these days. Garage girls, desultory nails, a crow-backed display. An experiment of wingspan.

The darkness of my answer to your sword

Not knowing is a way of pressing forward. I'm shadowed by the language of indefinites, unable to throw sharpened sights into their rightful relief. Breaths track your movement, a slow pulse beacons the rock of disbelief. We're waving to you here. Expecting atoms of your smile to reach us any day now. I'm stretching the terms of my contract and writing you down. But, like sunlight, you won't stay still.

Faith in a method of elusive grace.

PET SITTING

Your golden puppy dissipates distress.
Time has passed alright, but Elmo's tail
wags in zen essence of its own atoms,
a brace of universal zest, perfect choreography
of what's happened to have come along.

He was born to his own unknowing
some short while ago, a reincarnation
of any crazy energy — shy, but if you lie
flat on the towering bed, he's bound
to play. And there's no
conception that you shouldn't taste
a gamut of individual palms. This is,
after all, a celebratory gathering.
And I'm not allocating any brine.

SAINT TERESA CONTEMPLATES HER FUTURES

A grip of holly has its way with me;
I am thorned into acquiescence.

You are there, nestling, as time allows
music and verse, and the fullness of bread.
Everything we think has well-earned tracks
for a smooth, short journey. Telling
looseness in the soil of it. Dug up growth.

I could rest here in the garden,
watching the birds breathe, the water
like a fourway prayer in its rise and fall.

The flash spread of tendrils shocks me.
Yet natural flowering, easy snaking
lulls in its non-discernible rhythm,
making the offering mine.

Intervals of lucent enclosure;
safety for the sake of tasting safety,
grass and sunlight battling odds
and ends of the earth we rest on.

News is a foil for restitution.
The stillness of amber, warm wood
sustaining externality of love—
feasts, passion, intimations that I carry
a purpose in continuing this way.

News is pinned to boards for intercession,
rotas are exceptionally kind, arranging
expectant displays of goodwill,
the easy blooms of summer,
honesty's silvery sense.

You're editing some days
and nothing can scratch you.
shoots of butter yellow creeping up
and a hint of luck.

SOME EXCUSES FOR LEAVING EARLY

You've been treading oranges
until your feet tango.

I can't abide the miasma of citrus peel,
all those bioflavonoids of flesh,
creating infinite aroma.
                        Snarl
is my one reaction to refreshment.
I'd rather winter on
                  this continent, grub
around for small enchantments.
Await my hundredth birthday
snuffling in sleepish apertures
replete with various seeds.

Since you live at random on my edge
I'd like to offer you confabulations.

Hallucinating blankets yet again.
It's a cardboard brain, all in all,
tough, but in a mood to get
soggy. Slashed apart, made to recoup
with lashes of brown tape.

Just a bland translation
of a calming verse
holding me the way I like it.

Code of the potential winner's
planted in the genesis of green:
should he take the rap upon the hand,
flummoxed by opera? Should I demand
an assurance of love, take a statement?
The sigh of the comforted land.

The charge to arrive makes you think
you should stay for a while.
You dance to the record, allowing
an unknown partner to settle the score.

Rubber Club

No shunting me on a rotary. Hooplas
as you lean to the cleavage and slip
like the classical ghost of a father, on ice.
Benificence clichés your second name.
You don't know what's cupping my hearts
in the red; but I'm half-cut with a pad
on each knee, acres of linen in my esoteric mouth,
and I chew up religions, intent on the central
menu. You can't guess what I'm spying on.
You, with your gusset-lined hands, wounded
by out-of-hours office, the taste of a finger
in her clear bowl of soup. Like candy, I spot you.
These walls were made for bouncing, this
table for spilling the sauce, like sand in a fist.
Dry my clean sheet with the laundry list; I'm
looping an ardour by pecking you. Outside,
the weavers spin, the thin girls clasp their clipboards
and put you down as lost. The taxi waits
with my friend inside. Loose canon, your
lecherous flattery batters my thighs.

CAT'S CRADLE

Born in a net of sapphires, the spiritual
baby delivers her saws. Angels in the throat?
Then cough when I get the right answer.
Don't go splitting the wires you fly by, the
lessons of sassy despair and the interim tests.
Count days on your toes. Fish for the deeper
depression, the stars and the squids can do battle
at home. And I bless your wet pickings, the look
in those diamond green eyes and the rub of your head
on my sleeve. Scamper up to the hot
bowl of tea. You understand my tastes.
These bars outside my house are fit for men.
The window is wide just a slit, just a sip
for the shadowed morning torso. You
could propose at a price like this, drop
a line of intention's industrial train. Flutter
the lace of an old maid's eyes. *I did not
survive.* I did not survive the ineffable type
of your circus desertion. Yet the stroke
of a purr — and I'll tell it all over again.

MEDITATION TOPICS FOR WOMEN

1. If a bird wishes to join the sisters for meditation, but can't follow the office hymns, what is one to do?

2. If there are twelve sisters presently resident, why do there sometimes seem twice this many at 5pm meditation?

3. If a sister should suddenly seem drunk and eager to sit only in sunshine, should this be permitted?

4. If one suspects a sister has red wine in her cell, should one visit her in the hope of being offered a glass?

5. If the slim tabby cat wishes to join the sisters and the bird for meditation, where should she sit?

6. If the mother superior offers each of the sisters a small wildflower from the grounds, is it customary to offer one back?

7. Should the statue of Our Lady cry, which sister should offer an apology?

8. If a sister should levitate, is it prudent to take photographs?

9. Should a priest vanish at the altar, must cleaning be postponed?

10. How many sisters does it take to change an altar cloth?

11. How many suppers does it take to fill a sister's bones with health?

12. How many palm crosses does it take to build a workable two-sister raft?

Printed in the United Kingdom
by Lightning Source UK Ltd.
108892UKS00001B/260